I0478586

# What Changed Our Lives

# What Changed Our Lives

*An Expat Adventure*

RUDOLF HARTONG

authorHOUSE®

*AuthorHouse™ UK Ltd.*
*1663 Liberty Drive*
*Bloomington, IN 47403  USA*
*www.authorhouse.co.uk*
*Phone: 0800.197.4150*

*© 2013 by Rudolf Hartong. All rights reserved.*

*No part of this book may be reproduced, stored in a retrieval system, or transmitted by any means without the written permission of the author.*

*Published by AuthorHouse  10/24/2013*

*ISBN: 978-1-4918-8310-5 (sc)*
*ISBN: 978-1-4918-8311-2 (e)*

*This book is printed on acid-free paper.*

*Because of the dynamic nature of the Internet, any web addresses or links contained in this book may have changed since publication and may no longer be valid. The views expressed in this work are solely those of the author and do not necessarily reflect the views of the publisher, and the publisher hereby disclaims any responsibility for them.*

This booklet is based on the real story of an expatriate family with five children.

For Arjan, Michelle, Shinta, Kyle, and Emily

# PREFACE

This book describes the experiences of our family, composed of a mother and father with five children, who kept moving around the world, living over time in seven different countries. Each time one of our children finished high school, having been studying for the International Baccalaureate, being eighteen or nineteen years old, we had to say goodbye to them, as they continued their studies in another country (and sometimes in another language). As parents, this was not always an easy period, but that is also the case for every parent who is not living an expatriate life but who has to say goodbye to a child who moves away from home; the same feelings are involved. Having accepted our last assignment (in country number seven), we found ourselves starting life as a couple again, as we did when we were just married.

We have learned a lot, and we have experienced many situations which we would like to share with you in these pages. Each country that we resided in is of course different from any other, as it is also determined by time and place, but there are many experiences to share.

Each of our five children will explain about his or her personal experiences—positive and negative—in Chapter 6 ("Let Our Children Speak"): Each of our children discusses at what age and how he or she started the expatriate life as well as how he or she coped with what the change brought. I felt it was better to let them explain in their own words what they felt and what they did in this important part in their lives.

Now, as all of them are married or have partners, and as they are spread around the world (which is a consequence of the life that we chose to live), we offer this book to their partners to—I hope—enable them to better understand the lives that our sons and daughters lived during their younger years.

Before I go any further, I would like to clarify the term "expatriate", because it can cause some confusion nowadays. According to the dictionary: "An expatriate is someone who lives in a country which is not their own." (Source: BBC, English Dictionary. Harper Collins Publishers.) That is the meaning behind my use of the word in this publication. In some organisations, European people moving inside of the European Union (EU) are not called "expatriates" any more but are rather referred to as "transferees" or as "short-term assignment contractors". For me, they are also expatriates because these people move to different cultures and often to different language situations.

Maybe their financial compensation package has been changed with the creation of the EU and will often be based on the same level as their European colleagues (or maybe a bit more), but much less than moving to a hardship country or a country in an emerging market. Often people in Europe who stay in a country that is not their own for a long time cannot be called "expatriates" any more, as they have adapted themselves to the culture and the language of the country that they are now living in. This development you see also in hardship countries or emerging markets where expatriates and their families live for many years and become "local". Sometimes they marry a local person and have a family in the country to which they moved. Often multinational companies use the term "expatriate" when the employee has been staying in the same country for a certain length of time—typically up to five or seven years. After that, the person is considered to have become "local", and his or her financial compensation package will be based on local compensation norms. It can differ from country to country, financial compensation being also based on the laws in the country. Some countries have special tax regulations for expatriates, for example, tax deductions of up to 25 per cent. You can obtain relevant information from your international human resources department and from the embassy of the country to which you plan to move. The Internet, and particularly search engines such as Google for example, is a helpful information tool.

In my earlier published book, *General Management for Operational Managers* (published May 23, 2013, by AuthorHouse), I wrote a small chapter concerned with how to settle in as a family in a new country. This book, however, goes into much greater detail on this subject and covers the whole range of experience from starting in a new country until the moment that the children leave home. Each move means a loss of valuable emotional memories and experiences, which is the case for everybody who moves. It is painful to say goodbye to colleagues you worked with—sometimes in difficult circumstances—and to friends with whom you bonded very closely in a school. As the title to this work suggests, it changed our lives.

Rudolf Hartong
September 2013

# ACKNOWLEDGEMENTS

I would very much like to thank Annette Dill-Andree, Rose Gan, Cameron Skandarioon, Barbara and Hendrik Wittenberg, my wife, Johanna, our children, and my in-laws for their valuable contributions, comments, and reactions that have made this book what it is now.

Johanna took the pictures that appear in this book.

# TABLE OF CONTENTS

Preface . . . . . . . . . . . . . . . . . . . . . . . . . . vii

Acknowledgements . . . . . . . . . . . . . . . . . . . . . xi

Chapter 1: Before Accepting a Position Abroad . . . . . . . . . . 1

    1.1     Considerations . . . . . . . . . . . . . . . . . . 1
    1.2     The Preparation. . . . . . . . . . . . . . . . . . 4
    1.3     The Children . . . . . . . . . . . . . . . . . . 12

Chapter 2: Change of Countries . . . . . . . . . . . . . . . 20

    2.1     One Works; One Stays at Home . . . . . . . . 20
    2.2     Our Experiences . . . . . . . . . . . . . . . . 22
    2.3     The Next Move. . . . . . . . . . . . . . . . . 22
    2.4     Our Moves . . . . . . . . . . . . . . . . . . . 24

Chapter 3: Culture (Shock) . . . . . . . . . . . . . . . . . 26

    3.1     The Mindset . . . . . . . . . . . . . . . . . . 26
    3.2     Our Experiences . . . . . . . . . . . . . . . . 28
    3.3     Intercultural Influences. . . . . . . . . . . . . 33

Chapter 4: "Spoiled" Children . . . . . . . . . . . . . . . . 36

Chapter 5: What can Happen after Your Children Leave Home? . . 40

Chapter 6: Let Our Children Speak . . . . . . . . . . . . . . 43

    6.1     Suzanne. . . . . . . . . . . . . . . . . . . . . 43
    6.2     Maarten. . . . . . . . . . . . . . . . . . . . . 48
    6.3     Frank . . . . . . . . . . . . . . . . . . . . . . 51

6.4    Irene . . . . . . . . . . . . . . . . . . . . . . 58

6.5    Paul . . . . . . . . . . . . . . . . . . . . . . . 63

Chapter 7: Citizens of the World . . . . . . . . . . . . . . . . 71

"Citizen of the World": a song by Ellis Paul . . . . . . . . . . 75

About the Author . . . . . . . . . . . . . . . . . . . . . . 81

# CHAPTER 1

## Before Accepting a Position Abroad

### 1.1 Considerations

Before you accept a position abroad, it is important to consider why you may wish to move abroad. Below are some common reasons:

> Do you wish to move because of the money? Yes, it could be. In general, expatriate jobs are better paid than jobs in your home country, but the position will also ask and demand more of you and your family. It is important to not underestimate the implications of taking a position abroad because of the economic opportunities.
>
> Are you leaving because you would be moving into a job that represents a higher position and carries higher status? Are you looking for a new challenge or to prove yourself for instance in an emerging market? These are all reasonable and fair arguments, but you have to realise that

if you go back to your home country and/or your home organisation after a couple of years, the people there are unlikely to understand what sort of experiences you have had, and you may well be offered at this point the same job as you had before, not a higher position. It is possible that you will not have a job to return to at all! Disillusion and disappointment can result. It is better to realise this before you leave.

On this issue, it is important also to realise that your family and friends in your home country will not be aware of many of the challenges and adventures that you and your family have experienced while being abroad. So, when coming home, you can discover a "gap" between what you experienced and what they experienced in the home country during the period that you were away. You may find that some family members and friends avoid you, as they think that you are not the same any more (that may well be the case, as a move abroad will change you).

It is worth giving contemplation before you move abroad to whether you want to keep your roots in your native country alive for yourselves and your children. You may be able to keep your house in your native country or later on buy a summer house/holiday home in your home country where you and your children can go and feel at home in order to keep the contacts and roots alive and maintain a close relation to your family and friends. That is a very important decision to make because it affects the selection of the right school system for your children. Be aware that you should keep the family's native language/

mother tongue alive. This can be done by participating in special clubs and/or by having a place on an extra-curricular language programme. To keep up speaking the native language at home will avoid alienation and possible disadvantage at school if your children return to their native country.

Is it because you see it as being a way to save your marriage/partnership? If your relationship is not solid, an escape to another country is unlikely to solve any problems. In fact, I have frequently seen a move abroad end up in a divorce. No, the partnership should have a solid base. If that is the case then a move to another country can make the relationship even stronger. Remember that you are settling in a new country, with new rules, a different culture, and perhaps the use of a language that you do not speak; you and your partner will need to survive this together. It is an experience that can create extra bonding: "Together we must do it. We must manage and accept the new environment. We have to develop new friendships. We have to stand on our own feet."

Is it an adventure? Do you want to see the world? Someone's decision to move abroad can be rooted in an old desire to see more of the world. It can also be an attempt to escape routine or boredom in the actual situation. Be aware that it should be not only you or your wife who decides to move but the whole family together.

Do you want to settle in a different country to give your children the possibility of learning another language and culture or to give them an opportunity to have the "living abroad experience"? Some parents like us, if they get this opportunity, think that it could give their children an extra experience and therefore dimension in their lives by living abroad and getting to know other cultures.

In general, it is a difficult process to evaluate what could be the positive impact of a new position abroad as well as possible negative consequences. It can be an emotional process of saying farewell to a house, pets, neighbours, family members, and many valuable experiences, even while knowing that you will retain many good memories and should be enjoying a new home and so on. It is a kind of emigration. If you have the answers to the considerations above, then prepare yourself, as we did, by making lists of steps that you will have to take before you actually move.

## 1.2    The Preparation

What should you expect and how should you prepare for it? Visit your local bookshops and library and read books and articles about the city or country that you plan to live in. There are specialised guides, such as those produced by Berlitz, containing maps, phrases, and lists of attractions. Use the Internet to research information on the shopping centres and the leisure facilities. Talk to people who live or have lived in that country. Visit cultural seminars and/or workshops organised by institutes and organisations about living in another country. You can also write to or otherwise contact the embassy of the planned new country if you would like to clarify any particular issues beforehand; for sure, they should be willing to help you with all kinds of information.

When a transfer is planned to a country where they do not speak your mother tongue, it is especially advisable that you and your family members spend time at home before the move learning about the history, culture, and language of that country. Depending on their ages, you may find that you struggle to motivate your children to take an interest (as they have other interests), but at least you and your partner can make an effort. We encouraged our children to learn some English before we took our first job abroad. The two eldest children managed this task, but the others were simply too young to understand the importance of it. But when school had started one of the youngest stood on stage, after two months, in an English language play. When we moved to Moscow, Russia, we told our two teenagers that they were not allowed to go out if they could not master the Russian alphabet. The names of the metro stations were at that time only given in Russian. They studied hard!

There are in existence many institutes that provide cultural seminars as well as many schools and training centres that provide language courses via the Internet or through classes. In most countries the residents speak at least some English, or something that sounds like English, and with some learning, you will probably be able to work with that and adapt yourself to the situation.

## Visiting the Country

A visit to the future country and company/organisation before you finally accept the offer is often offered by the organisation and can help you and your family to make the final decision. Even if you have had many short visits to the new country and you think you know it all, it will be different if you settle in that place for a longer period.

Have in mind that for you as a single person, a couple, or a family, despite all of the preparations that you may be making in advance, the reality will always be a little different. When we moved to Indonesia with our small dog, we reserved a hotel and included the dog in that reservation. However, when it came to actually checking in, we found that the dog was not allowed, because of Muslim culture. You really do not know exactly, or you will only realise afterwards, what you are getting yourself into. This is not necessarily negative, but you need to recognise that in the decision phase you will be looking at the offer and the situation with different eyes than when you are actually at the final location. That is human. Compare it with a new job and the interviews you had for that job. When you arrive in your new position, things often turn out differently from what you had expected during the interviews. Feeling homesick, unexpected cultural differences and a situation where your partner does not find work or a position equal to what he or she had in your home country could play a role when you finally settle in. However, your enthusiasm and determination and your view of it as a challenge for you and your family members will make it an enjoyable experience and a success. Have in mind that it is not a holiday, and not every country you were offered is as nice or as agreeable as you had hoped for, but after all that is why you took up the challenge. You may find yourself in a hardship country with political and social unrest, earthquake risks, or very hot or very cold temperatures or in a very poor country where good infrastructure is lacking. The more difficult the situation, however, then the bigger that the challenge will be, and the success that you can create for you and your employees can prove very rewarding. The positive attitude of you and your partner/family can bring, even in a hardship country, unforgettable, positive experiences, because of the local population, the colleagues, and the friends that you encounter.

A short checklist of areas of consideration when visiting the "new" country:

Political situation
History
Culture
Transportation systems
Housing situation
General health situation
Religious restrictions
School situation
Special laws to consider as a foreigner
Banking systems
Sport clubs and international clubs
Working visa/residence permit
Procedure for bringing in a pet, including vaccinations.

## Health

Prior to moving to another country, there are a few health matters that you should ask about. First, contact the health department in your organisation about the country you plan to move to. A local doctor or a specialised medical clinic can also give you all of the necessary information about vaccinations and medicines that are locally available or not. These precautions should be taken with the aim of making your stay in your new country a success and a pleasant experience. The basis of all of the considerations and decisions that you have to take (as well as should be taken by the organisation/

company that is planning your transfer) is the fact that both you and your partner are in good health. Often companies ask you to have a health check. Sometimes health problems can be a reason not to send you, if no good treatment possibilities are available in the assignment country or if the health risks for you or your partner are too big.

## Paperwork

What is also important is getting the necessary papers in order. Maybe you need to do some paperwork to get a working visa. Maybe you need a residence permit for you and your partner and/or children. You may wish to obtain information about the assigned country's tax system. It can be very beneficial to make a checklist with respect to administrative issues, but local or international human resources departments should be able to help you in these matters, and the receiving organisation may even be taking most of the work out of your hands in these respects.

## Family Considerations

After the decision is made to relocate there are some considerations for your family regarding an international move. When we left for our first country abroad (Spain), we decided to go for an international (English) school system, as we planned to stay abroad, if possible, for a few more years. (At the time we never expected that it would be for twenty-four years!) You can read Chapter 6 ("Let Our Children Speak") to obtain an idea of whether it was the right choice for our children. It is very difficult as it will affect the life and future of you, but also very much that of your children. You know what you do, but your children do not know; they follow their parents. Our children had a mixed reaction; some of them say that they lost their roots, which is correct. But what is done is done, and you cannot go back and do it again.

If possible, I always advise that the person who is taking up the expat position should move in a few months earlier than the other members of the family in order to prepare the home and to make some arrangements with, for example, schools. It will also give him or her the time to concentrate on the new job and to form an idea of the challenges that lie ahead.

Nowadays, when in many couples both partners have a job in order to contribute to the family income, the situation can be problematic, as in some countries only the assigned partner may be able to obtain a work permit. In some countries it is possible to find work for a partner, but in reality this may be difficult because of language problems and/or a big local unemployment situation. Your partner may have to make a very important decision to join you and maybe look for voluntary work (that could be very satisfactory and much appreciated and needed). A decision can be made not to join and to rather stay at home, with the idea that one or both travel to meet each other and spend some time together. The latter is a very difficult arrangement for sustaining a relationship, however, and most of the time it will not work. I would not advise such an option based on what I have heard and seen. Partners start with good intentions, but, often—although fortunately not always—it goes wrong. I can mention many examples where it went wrong and that cannot be the base of such an important decision to work abroad!

An example I experienced myself was when I was offered a position at the beginning of the 1990s in Moscow, Russia. At that time it was not considered very wise to move your family to Russia, because the political situation in the country was not very stable. As I knew the situation in Russia I asked to have a weekly flight home to my family outside of Russia. The request was not approved, and I turned the offer down. Later my management accepted my request. It was decided in cooperation with my company at that time to settle the family in Stockholm and that I should travel home every weekend (Moscow-Stockholm). I did this commute from Sweden to Russia for three years—every weekend. It was tough and difficult, also—for my wife and children as well as for me. However, we managed it, and it saved my marriage. Everybody has to make his or her choices and sacrifices.

## The Actual Move

The logical consequence of good preparation and making a final decision are decisions around the actual move. For consideration are the following issues:

Your housing situation in your home country. Do you rent out or sell your home?

Cancellation or postponement of all kinds of insurances, such as insurances of property and other belongings. (It is advisable to make a list.)

What do you want to bring with you when you move, and what do you want to leave behind? How will you move your possessions? Will you need local storage?

Selecting the right moving company. Normally the organisation will help you in this regard, and often they have contracts with international moving companies. Otherwise the Yellow Pages or the Internet should be able to provide you with a list of international moving companies.

Saying farewell to family and friends.

Checking if the tickets and other papers are in order for arrival in the new country.

Our personal experiences with international moving companies:

A particular point that I think worth mentioning is the loss of furniture and other belongings during moving to which members of my family were emotionally attached. There was not one move where we did not lose one or more items that had emotional value for us. In spite of the professionalism of international moving companies, they do not always seem to get this right. In the beginning we filed claims with the insurance company, but in reality that proved a hassle to settle and agree about the final amount of the claim and involved much correspondence and irritation, so later on we gave up and no longer filed any claims if something went missing. It was not worth the time and irritation. The moving companies do not seem to understand that in some cases you are not concerned about the material value of an item that is lost. I often told them that the material value of the item was nothing or next to nothing, but the emotional value of a stone, a picture, or a piece of furniture that hurts when it did not arrive at the new destination. For me the insurance premium is just an extra income for the moving companies, because for us (or the company who pays) it is a waste of money.

## 1.3    The Children

An important point to consider in deciding to move to another country is the age of your children if they are to accompany you. Small children can normally be easily taken with you, but from the age of about twelve children can start to put up some strong defences to a move. With tact and patience you can usually overcome most of their hesitations or even rebellious behaviour, but it can require a lot of attention from parents. Also there can be difficulties if you plan to move on again—perhaps several times—in the future, by accepting new foreign assignments. Being together in a foreign culture can make the family bond stronger, but breaking up bonds with friends usually needs a lot of talking and explaining, and children are likely to need help each time to settle down and form new bonds.

Your children will likely discover later as they get new friends in a new country that their friends will have made similar experiences. These contacts will be less intense, because their school friends know and your child knows that in the next school year they may not see each other because they have moved or you will have moved again. That is both positive and negative, but a consequence of the life you and your children have chosen. It will give them a completely different vision of the world compared with the one that they would have had if they had stayed at home. It will also result in a more isolated life, as real friendship and bonding is much more difficult. At a certain age, young children need the strong bonds, and that can cause a problem.

For teenagers it can be a challenge in some countries to relax in the same way that they were used to doing in their previous environment. Going out is sometimes not possible, or not possible in the same ways, because of security reasons, so they tend to find themselves sticking together and having parties at home or at certain special clubs or attending hotel discos. My wife on many occasions invited a large group of young boys and girls to our home, where they could relax and enjoy themselves together. Sport—formally organised or otherwise—is also a nice way to let the teenagers relax and have fun.

The use of (too much) alcohol or drugs is not new in this environment, but that is also a problem in schools in your home country. The difference is that in some countries, the penalties can be very severe, including the death penalty. So it is a task of the international school and the parents to keep an eye on it and to control it, but that is never 100 per cent possible. I know of one case in which a young child was caught by the police in a bar using drugs. What followed was an immediate suspension of the child from the school, and the father, who was a diplomat in the country, had to leave the country to avoid punishment. So this teenager ruined his father's career.

Freedom is a relative concept in such sensitive countries, and your children should be aware of it. To compensate for that, these beautiful countries often have other challenges for youngsters to explore. Sometimes the international schools organise trips for their students. For example in Denmark, there was a trip to the Sami people in the north of Scandinavia. In Moscow, there was rafting and camping alongside Lake Baikal and a trip to Sochi. The sea and the mountains, as well as the traditions and the warm and welcoming people, should make the young people's stay an unforgettable one and leave a lasting impression. It will form them into citizens of the world.

*Education*

If you have children, you and your partner will have to think about the school(s) that you want to select for your children to attend, if you can select. Do you want a school where they speak your native language? This is not a possible option in all countries, but sometimes you can find such schools. This may be especially important to you if your assignment is only for a few years and after that time you will return to your home country. Or, if available, would you prefer an international school? You will need to discover the curriculum that the school is following. They may be teaching British A levels, or they may be teaching the International Baccalaureate Diploma Programme (IBDP or IB).

The British A level system is currently covering social science education and a public examination in a subject taken for the General Certificate of Education (GCE) usually at the age of seventeen or eighteen years, plus the course leading to this examination and A level maths. For details: Google British A-levels

The International Baccalaureate Diploma Programme is a two-year educational programme primarily aimed at students aged sixteen to nineteen years that provides an internationally accepted qualification for entry into higher education and that is recognised by many universities worldwide. For further details, see http://en.wikipedia. org/wiki/IB_Diploma_Programme

Often your company or organisation and their international human resources department can give you some information about the future country and the schooling system in that country. When you engage in an orientation visit to the country and city in which you plan to settle, you can visit schools and discuss the possibilities of programmes and examinations with your child or children.

If you have decided to follow an international school system, you have to realise that there are, in general, no special attention programmes for children who are in need of particular care; it follows *one* programme for everybody. As I always say, your children do not have to be Einsteins, but they need to have a normal intelligence so they can follow these school systems. If your children need special medical attention or extra support with their studies then consider whether it is wise to continue with such an international assignment. In one case I saw, one of the partners took that voluntary job and supported their child at home with extra attention and help. It worked in that case. Otherwise, it will probably be very difficult, both for you and, especially, for your child. Then it is better to reconsider such a planned move.

In the seven countries that we lived in, our children went to different schools but in most cases to international schools, preparing for the International Baccalaureate exam, comparable to a kind of senior high school. In Stockholm, they went to an English school. Our son attended a local French language primary school in Lausanne, Switzerland. In Copenhagen, Denmark, our two oldest children received some extra-curricular Dutch language lessons, which were, however, not a success. The level of programmes and exam results of international schools vary a lot, and, where you have options available to you, you should investigate each institution thoroughly. Talk to parents and teachers to help you to form your own opinions. If the level of the establishment does not seem to be what you expected, but you have no choice in where to send your child, you could consider organising some extra tuition for your child or help your children yourself if possible. While not wishing to discredit any of the many schools that our children followed, the best school and the best experience that we had was with the United Nations School in Hellerup in Copenhagen. Their school level of programmes at that time was very good, and the exam results were nearly 100 per cent! On top of that, the atmosphere at the school stimulated the children very much. For children, the school in a foreign country is more than just a school; it is a period of great development for them, especially if they are of sixteen to eighteen years and bonding with others. Friendships are very important at that age. It must be the best period of their school life!

We have described the situation when you have chosen to keep your children with you on your assignments. Sometimes this is not possible because of the situation in the country. It can also be a tradition in a family to send the children to a boarding school, which could be in the country where the expat is living, or it could be back in their home country, often with the argument that they want the children to keep their roots in the country where they will be studying in the long term later on, so the change for the child is not too big. It often happens that a child who has studied abroad and obtained a diploma there is then sent back to his or her home country to study at a college or a university. Unfortunately, it happens frequently that these young people feel themselves to be strangers in their own country. This is something that we experienced with two of our children when they got their IB diplomas and then went back to Holland for university study. Our daughter was treated and guided very well at the university that she attended, for example, receiving extra lessons in Dutch and being allowed extra time during exams to make use of a dictionary, and she managed. Our son, however, did not receive this extra support at the university that he attended and was completely confused between the Dutch and English language. He found out that he could not understand complicated Dutch terms in the study material for his course, such as the meaning of "a square equation" when given in Dutch, he felt that he could not cope with it. It became a failure, and he had to change for a college, which worked out well for him. For us, that was the reason to send our three younger children to colleges and universities in the United Kingdom and Switzerland after finishing their IB courses. It is thus very difficult as to what to advise in this respect; it is a very personal choice as to what determines this decision, and it is acknowledged that many variables will come into play, not restricted to: family tradition, the wishes of the children, and the situation in the country where you will live.

Education: What comes after international school?

What is the next step after your son or daughter has finished his or her studies at an international school, doing A levels, or having been studying for the IB? Where should they go to continue to study if they should so wish?

Most of these children will continue their studies. If they have decided what to study, then it becomes a joint effort between the parents and these young adults to look for the right college or university. It is essential to take into account the costs while recognising the possibilities of grants, scholarships, and other sources of financial support. Grants are not always available, and the family may have to take the costs, which may be quite high. It is important that your son or daughter is motivated in his or her study choice. If he or she is not so motivated, even after consulting professional study advisors, it is better to wait. I know some young people who took a year off from studying and who went backpacking, earning money during their trip. The time afforded them the opportunity to make up their mind as to what course they wished to enrol on.

It is advisable to start the discussions about the future of your child during the last year of their schooling, or even earlier, because often a visit to a college or a university is needed to see the surroundings, feel the atmosphere, meet the right people, and mutually make a decision. I have always experienced these discussions and visits as very valuable, not just with respect to children's future plans but especially as they concern the relation with your grown-up child. You come to a better understanding of each other through this time together, and this is important, as he or she will soon leave you. Remember that the visits will need to fit into your own (travel) programmes, and they may have to be scheduled for the school holidays, as the only large block of time available in which to travel.

Once the decision has been made then you and your child can largely focus on the school exam, although a few issues may remain to be dealt with, such as living accommodation for the next few years. Depending on the study choice, some colleges or universities offer campus systems, where the students live and study close to or even on the university compound. Others do not have such arrangements and then can start the hassle of finding a room somewhere or a student apartment.

Boarding possibilities are available in some universities and colleges, but sometimes this is only an option for the first year. Related to this process is the very important decision of whether to study in your original home country or not. This decision is important, because if your child decides not to do that then the chance that your child will move back later on, after his or her studies are finished, is small. By this point they will likely speak the local language and be willing and able to find a first job in that country. They may well meet somebody who they wish to live with locally. They may even be happy to start moving around. The world is open for them—you have shown them that yourself.

# CHAPTER 2

## Change of Countries

### 2.1 One Works; One Stays at Home

In Chapter 1, I mentioned the situation of two working partners moving to a new country where one of them takes the expatriate job and the related monetary compensation, and the remaining partner tries to look for a job, be it a paid job or a voluntary position. It depends of course on the country that the couple is moving to. Inside Europe the situation is normally not that complicated because of the European Union (EU) regulations, although high unemployment and what may be a new language can make it difficult. In emerging markets, besides the possible language problem, sometimes the governments do not allow both partners to work and have restrictions for granting working visas. Working visas are normally given based on education and experience in the position, when a local person cannot fulfil the position at that moment in time in that country. I experienced people staying at home and taking care of the children and doing voluntary work. In some hardship countries I heard from people getting a job at the embassy of their country and sometimes at the company of their partner, because staying at home on their own during the day in what they knew was a very difficult local situation is not always a good solution. A job was sometimes created to keep the expatriate.

The partner who has not taken the expatriate job will have very important tasks. To mention a few:

> Helping and supporting the working partner
> Receiving company guests
> Organising dinners
> Looking after the children (teenagers especially can have difficulties in countries where their movements are restricted)
> Looking after the household staff

This all is needed to run the household smoothly. On top of these, there are many other possibilities in many countries, for example, being involved in sporting activities and voluntary work like visiting orphanages, helping in schools with extra lessons, being a nurse or a medical advisor (if you are trained as a medical doctor) and visiting sick people.

Frequently, rewarding and long-lasting friendships develop out of these situations, and they can remain for many years, even after you have left the country. It is important that he or she feels motivated and respected and sees his or her work as being of benefit to themselves in terms of their personal development and as an important contribution to the country that they are living in.

## 2.2  Our Experiences

If the long-term plan is to move on to other countries, and if this way of living is appreciated, the partners at home normally automatically find their way in a new society in the next country. In our case, with five growing children, my wife was very busy taking care of the children's daily needs, visiting schools, and helping our children—and sometimes their classmates—with their homework as the level of each international school is not the same unfortunately. In the last two assignments, she studied Russian, and after a few years she could write, read, and speak this difficult language, which helped her a lot. In Indonesia she learned the language, too, alongside taking care of the household staff, receiving guests from the company who visited our home, and volunteering at the Museum Nasional (the National Museum of Indonesia) in Jakarta, first as a trained guide for foreign visitors and later as a trainer, preparing new guides. All of this contributed to her satisfaction and personal development.

## 2.3  The Next Move

If you have taken an assignment abroad then it is very important during your stay in the country to be giving thought as to what you would like to do once your contract has finished. I suggest that you start working on that question at least one year before your contract expires. Can you and do you want to extend your stay?

What is the situation in the organisation or company? Do they want to expand more internationally, and do you want to take part in that? How have you been fulfilling this assignment? Has it been a success thus far? Is the company happy and satisfied with your performance? Was it worth the money that they spent on you and your family? I know that these can be difficult questions to answer, especially if you live far away from the head office. You need to have a superior or other connection to the head office who can give you some feedback and answers to these questions. It is very important to be aware of the situation, as you want to avoid playing the wrong negotiation tactic; For instance, you can be demanding on your new position, but if the situation in the company is not good and not many expat positions are available, then you should perhaps be more prudent in your approach of a new position.

Out of these negotiations, depending on your and your partner's flexibility, but also related to the eventual new location, you may receive a new offer—a new challenge. With respect to how we handled it, the pattern we developed was that towards the end of my contract each time our children would typically ask the same questions: Are we staying here longer? Will our contract be extended, or do we have to prepare for the next move? We would have a family meeting around the table and discuss the options and eventual next move and related job offer. The next job offer will not always represent a promotion; it could be a different function. You have to be aware of this and be flexible enough to accept it and to see the challenge that it will bring. I have moved from being a managing director to become a (general) manager and vice versa. I have seen my salary grow, but I have also seen it go down by as much as 50 per cent (because of tax reasons).

When possible, we planned a visit to the city we were planning to relocate to in the new country and eventually visited the planned new school(s). In that way, my partner and the children were able to form opinions, which made our decisions easier, and for the children it became a matter of committing to the next move. Whenever a decision was taken on relocation, we first concentrated on finding the right school(s). Based on that decision, we looked for the right housing (with my wife having the most important say in that). My workplace and the distance to our home were the last things that I worried about. I reasoned that if my family was settled in the right way then it would be worth any extra time driving to and from the office.

## 2.4   Our Moves

Our first international move as a family was a move that happened quite late in my career. I was forty-one when we started living in Spain (Madrid). A very good time we had in Madrid with our family as we were all together. The job was a real challenge, as not many people I was coming into contact with at that time spoke English, so I had to learn Spanish fast. The next move was to Switzerland (Lausanne), where we planned as a family to stay for at least three years, but, because of changes in the company I was working for, we moved after only one and a half years—to Denmark (Copenhagen). For the children, that particular move proved difficult; they did not even have ample opportunity to say goodbye to their newly made friends.

In Denmark, we stayed for three years. Two of our children completed their IB exams, and they left home for further studies. For our two oldest the period in Denmark was their best time in the school, as they told us. From Denmark we moved to Sweden (Stockholm), a country in which we also stayed for three years. Our three children who were still living with us at this point had a very good time in Sweden, and my wife also enjoyed the life in Stockholm very much. Unfortunately, I was travelling back and forth every weekend from

*What Changed Our Lives*

a position in Moscow, so the educational and emotional support of our younger children at this time was mainly on her shoulders. But she managed! The eldest child in the house (number three) left after he got his IB diploma in Stockholm, and so there were only four of us when I took my next assignment in Holland (Leeuwarden) in the north of the country. Back to our home country.

As we planned to stay for only three years in Holland, the two children stayed in the international school system. After Holland, we moved together to Moscow, for a period of six years. It was a very interesting time in a booming country. After two years, and upon finishing her IB, our daughter left us. Our youngest son stayed for two years longer, and he enjoyed the life in Moscow. He left us with his IB diploma, and my wife and I stayed the last two years together in Moscow. For my last assignment, we moved to another country, Indonesia (Jakarta), where we stayed for another six years. That is how we made up our twenty-four years abroad until my retirement age.

Moving is accepting "loss": a loss of friends, colleagues, and a country, which you will miss. People often asked us which country we liked best, and the answer is a difficult one to give. The experience of a country was not only determined by that country but also by the children who were living at home with us and their ages at that time. With regard to the countries themselves, in one country we liked the countryside very much; in another country, we appreciated the safety and security; in another, we liked the rich culture; and in another we enjoyed the climate. So I really cannot give you the answer to this question, but all of them changed our lives as well as the lives of our children.

# CHAPTER 3

# Culture (Shock)

## 3.1    The Mindset

Moving to another country means always moving to another culture (possibly, but not always, giving you a cultural shock), because the people in that country have built their unique local culture over many years. Even moving inside your own country can bring you a different cultural experience, such as moving between the north and south of Sweden or the United Kingdom—not to mention the differences in big countries such as Russia, China, or India between the northern and southern, and the eastern and western, regions. The United States presents many examples of different cultures, in the separate states. And it is not only the cultures that vary, but also the languages that can be different. There is, for example, in existence more than 500 different languages and dialects in Indonesia.

So moving from one country to another means preparing for and accepting differences, including different customs and different situations. You have to understand that, and you have to be prepared to make concessions and adapt to the new situation, a reality many immigrants experience on a daily basis. This counts for you also. That should be a basic condition, if you want to make a success of your stay in another country. Anyone who is not prepared to take on such a challenge should reconsider before signing the new contract.

To do this, you prepare yourself and your partner and family for the cultural differences or even what some may call a cultural shock, that is, the customs and traditions that you are not used to and that you may (initially) find difficult to understand and deal with. If you do not prepare yourself beforehand then it will probably take a long time to accept a culture, or it may even be that you are never able to adapt to some elements of the culture in which you are living. Detailed below are some examples of cultural aspects that you may encounter, depending on the country:

- Men kissing one another, including a man kissing you, because you have become close friends

- The protocol of handshakes among all employees (in some countries, except to women) you meet as part of the daily routine

- Tribal-related traditions and religious customs

- Dinner with frequent drinking to celebrate business relations

- Joining the use of the sauna. After a business meeting I was invited by the customer to go to the sauna, and there he gave me a massage and expected that I would do the same for him.

- Also, the sensitive procedure with respect to handing over business cards is important to know.

- The consumption of alcohol is a highly sensitive matter in regions where it is forbidden by religion.

## 3.2   Our Experiences

As a family, we had a strong acceptance of diverse cultural elements, but we had certain difficulties in dealing with some of them. To mention a few:

Heavy drinking during negotiations
The lack of planning, especially related to the future
The way that citizens were handled at times by the local police and/or military, which we found at times to be quite brutal. We experienced that when we saw demonstrations and at police checkpoints.

I will relate below certain experiences that we had in the different countries in which we lived. It should be born in mind, however, that the more that you move around, the easier it becomes to adapt to other cultures and customs.

In **Spain,** we experienced an extremely hot climate in the summers. We had the custom that our children could choose what to do on their birthdays. Our daughter's birthday is in August, and she wanted to go for a walk in the woods. So we did. We drove to the woods around

Madrid, got out of the car, walked for two minutes and then ran back to the car, as it was extremely hot, and we did not think that it was possible to walk in the high temperature. The siesta was needed to survive the heat. The easygoing attitude of many of the locals, especially in the small villages, was one of the main attractions of Spain. We enjoyed the official dressing tradition when you go out in the evening for dinner. Everywhere we saw signs that this was a Catholic country, especially during the week before Easter, the so-called *Semana Santa* (Holy Week).

In **Switzerland**, we met people who are proud of their country. "Organised in the Swiss way" is a well-known expression. The Swiss have a very strong sense of independence, and they are accustomed to direct democracy, although they can be reluctant to accept cultural changes. They keep alive their own developed, typical Swiss culture, which you can experience in many villages and cantons, especially on 1 August, their National Day.

In **Denmark**, we experienced a feeling of security, a feeling of openness, and a people who are proud of their country and of what they have achieved. Equality between men and women can be seen in many aspects of the organisation of the society. They are also more relaxed than in many other countries.

In **Sweden**, we experienced cold temperatures in the north and a formal dress code when visiting people at their home. People tend to live closely with their families and friends and stick largely to them. Like in Denmark, nearly all men and women of working age are working, so a good system of childcare is available. Sweden is a very well-developed country while also being one that is rich in history, with many original and typical small churches. Photographing them became my wife's hobby; we have an album at home with many pictures of beautiful, small churches in different architectural styles. The nature of the Stockholm area is very beautiful, and you can walk for hours in the woods without meeting anybody, except possibly a moose or a deer, and you can get lost on these ventures. Also the boat trips in the archipelago are an event that you will never forget.

**The Netherlands**, as our home country, should not have given us many cultural challenges. However, when we moved back to the Netherlands, we moved to the north, to a province called Friesland, where we had never lived before, and it is a province with its own recognised language, *Fries*, and with many typical traditions like "*fierljeppen*" (pole-vaulting across water), as well as the biggest ice skating tour in the world—the "*Elfsteden tocht*" (Eleven Cities Tour). Frieslanders are proud people, "stubborn" as they are proud to be called, but very nice and open people if you get to know them. Friesland has a picturesque, open countryside, where we enjoyed

*What Changed Our Lives*

discovering the many lakes and typical *skûtsjes* (special wooden boats)

**Russia** is already a culture on its own, having a very high standard of culture in ballet, music, and paintings in this biggest country of the world with a great number of different populations, languages, and cultures within its borders. Other noticeable characteristics include the vodka traditions, alcohol abuse (unfortunately), their warm people, and the enormous hospitality that you encounter, especially in the countryside. When you have made a friendship with a Russian, it remains for life. They love fur and fur coats; their girls are beautiful and very proud of their femininity and showing it off. They adore military uniforms and the military as an institution. They drive like madmen and cause many accidents. They are brave people. But corruption exists.

**Indonesia,** with its hot temperature, is likely to overwhelm you when you first come into the country. We adapted to the hot temperature by accepting the typical "shopping mall culture" (air conditioning) and by organising activities in the early morning or in the late evening. The warm and open people are always smiling and wanting to make you happy, which can cause some problems when you live there. We found that the taxi drivers may not know how to get you to your desired location, but they will assure you that everything is alright, because they want you to be happy. You may also frequently find yourself wondering how long it will take you to get somewhere because of the traffic jams. Once we went to the mountains, and the trip there took us about two hours by car, which we thought was acceptable, but the return journey took more than six hours by the same method of transport. We stopped making tours by car at the weekends. It is a very big country with many islands and different cultures and languages, developing very fast as you can see and experience everywhere. They have their special "home-made English language" which causes sometimes funny situations. For example, we found the following sign in a hotel bathroom: "This water tap is not for drinking". Superstition is still alive in a big part of this beautiful country. Indonesia is a moderate Muslim country with its rules and traditions. There is a shopping mall culture in the big cities. Corruption is alive. Many aspects of life can be organised.

Of course, this summing up is a personal reflection on our particular experiences at a particular time, and it can never—and it is not meant to—cover the whole culture of a country. The circumstances during the twenty-four years (1988-2012) of moving around may have changed since then. It shows, however, that you have to be prepared to accept cultural differences and sometimes a culture shock. You will have your own experiences, and you may think they are typical of a country where you lived for some time. It should be like that. It makes your life more interesting and makes you wise. The standards and norms from your home country are often not applicable in other situations. To see that will make you more tolerant and open to the acceptance of different opinions and cultures.

Another important aspect is the different races and religions you will encounter. It makes the picture of a country and your own experiences even broader. Take an interest in the different origins of the people, their history, languages, and traditions. You will meet very interesting people, some of whom may not have any higher education but have a great wisdom and interesting vision about life and their country. The same is true about religion. Why not discuss it and inform each other about religion? You will meet people who may know more about your religion than you know about theirs. Take the step, be open, and embrace the new country with its culture, and you will enrich yourself. It will change you, but what is wrong with that?

## 3.3    Intercultural Influences

Of course, there was a big intercultural influence in our personal lives but also in business.

### Our Personal Lives

Has our moving around changed us? A clear *yes* is the answer to this question, as you will have seen in reading the chapters prior to this one, and as you will very clearly see in Chapter 6, where our children provide their stories and impressions.

It has also changed my wife and me. The five children have five partners with different nationalities: one Dutch, one Philippine, one Indonesian, and two British. They also have different religions. For us, as parents, we much better understand our in-laws and their backgrounds because of our moving around and because of the influence on us of different cultures and religions. We have become more flexible, but also a little more passive, as we know that we cannot change everything ourselves. Also the partner choice is the choice of each of our children, and we support all of them.

We, but especially our children, have developed a special interest in other cultures. We all have developed a greater and better understanding of them, and we pick up the differences easier and adjust to them quite easily. You will recognise that after reading their stories. Our children are a good example of accepting and adjusting to cultural differences, as most of them continue to move around and live or have lived in countries like China, Mexico, and the United Arab Emirates (UAE) and in Europe. So for sure they learned their lessons and if needed are looking around for international work and other international opportunities.

## Business Influences

On a company level, many management styles are influenced by the Western ideology, based on the protestant/Calvinistic ideology of hard work, doing good, and the benefits that will come from this on earth and/or later in heaven that played a large role in the creation of capitalism. Later on it was balanced by a counter move of socialism. But it is still a Western-based philosophy which rules the business world. You can experience the Western-based philosophy in Asia and in Africa and in the emerging markets. The international accounting standard systems are implemented in big (multinational) Chinese or Russian companies as they are in companies thousands of miles away, and they will follow the same reporting and management computer systems. Many international companies are managing matters on the same principles. It more or less all looks the same.

Nonetheless, there are still cultural differences in doing business. The way you have to deal with your customer or supplier in Japan, the United States, Brazil, or Russia, to mention a few countries, differs a lot. But the language (English) used by the many big multinationals and how they administrate their business is becoming more and more uniform. Nonetheless, typical cultural differences fortunately remain, and you have to have an open eye for it. If not, it can give you a big surprise. Examples like the direct tough negotiations in Russia, where the personal relationship is very important, the lengthy negotiation strategies many Indonesian company owners follow, and as a contrast, the uncompromising rules of negotiations set by big multinationals.

Depending on the country and culture, as an expat you have to adapt and sort out the role that you have or want to play. In a company, it depends on the business situation; in schools, it depends on the set-up of the school/college/university, and it also depends on your age. You will probably find that you have to be able to play different roles at different times and in different situations, but that you will have learned during your long stay abroad. You must be able to—adapting yourself to be democratic or to be demanding. To negotiate and to give and take, roles all depending on the local situation and country and situation you come across.

# Chapter 4

## "Spoiled" Children

What I mean exactly with this use of the word "spoiled," I would like to explain to you. These children are not spoiled in the sense of having had too much attention—quite to the contrary. They had to learn, usually very early on in their lives, to stand on their own feet and to adapt to different cultures, languages, and sometimes difficult situations like extreme poverty, in the countries in which they lived. They have become very independent and have a ready tongue.

So in that sense they are not spoiled at all, but because of the different and sometimes difficult living situations (even living in a big house with household personnel), such as restrictions on their movements and following religious laws, having a different colour of the skin, they often felt themselves to be isolated and different from others around them. To make up for these circumstances, you may at times give them more material items like the latest films, items of home cinema equipment, computers, mobile phones, trips abroad (to really relax without the restrictions prevailing in some places), and a lot of other items and activities that you would not have been able to afford if you had continued to live in your home country.

As the children often follow an international schooling system that can be (very) costly, especially in the eyes of the local population, they will most likely meet classmates of similar economic and social standing, that is, children of embassy staff or children of captains of industry families, even children from a royal family. Those children, of course, do not represent a standard society. It is important to give your children a realistic vision of life; there is a world beyond the school world where you may find beggars, orphans, and poor people as well as well-educated locals. It is difficult to strike the right balance. Normally, the schools that your children will be attending will initiate activities like visits to less favourable situations and circumstances in which people have to live, or they may collect money for charities or organise to provide help, such as through a soup kitchen. Discussions and follow-up in class will normally follow to show the discrepancy between school life and the reality in the country.

As our children often did not speak the local language, it was not easy for them to find part-time work to do when they were about fifteen or sixteen years of age to earn their own pocket money. We felt that it was important to let them experience and understand the value of money, though; they were staying for (many) years in special living circumstances where money was never a problem. To let them know the value of money was something that we judged to be a very important element in their growing-up process; they needed to learn and know that by the time that they were leaving the international school at the age of eighteen or nineteen years.

Each child is different, but discussions about money and, if possible, doing some work to earn their pocket money, was very important. I remember when one of our children left home to study and after a few weeks he called his mother and said: "Mom, the month is longer than my money!" These situations happen, and they are a special memory now. It is a process for these children to get used to a completely new situation, to become self-reliant, when they leave home and are far away from their parents.

Wherever possible, depending on the country, we tried to organise together with our children some paid work when they were fifteen to sixteen years old. That ranged from distributing leaflets around the city/village (they could not speak the local language, but for distributing leaflets, you do not need that) to cleaning in offices and on aeroplanes to helping the local milkman on his daily route to working at a flower auction to working as a breakfast waiter in a hotel when they were seventeen to eighteen years old, to folding papers and leaflets at home (the whole family was involved). Our children still speak with enthusiasm of these activities. It helped to form them, and we also had fun doing it. To conclude this: Not all is bright sunshine and nice beaches and travelling around the world. These children reached a level of wisdom earlier, and they were possibly more alert than were children of the same age in their home country.

Our children in many senses had to become independent quite early on, as they often had to fight for themselves and felt isolated. This was not just an occurrence in the new country, but probably being

*What Changed Our Lives*

more spoiled materially and having seen more of the world than many others at times led to jealousy and a lack of understanding when they visited their home country during vacations. There was a gap with their peers at home that was not easy for them to understand or to overcome. Not all is as good as it seems.

# CHAPTER 5

## What can Happen after Your Children Leave Home?

You started together as a couple, and you have now arrived in the situation that it is again just the two of you. If you are still living and working abroad then this situation can give you new chances and opportunities; you are free to travel and to maybe take on a new assignment in a complicated situation, a challenge that may benefit from your rich experience. So a new period of adventures can be developed; plans, ideas, and dreams you could not realise before can become real.

During the years of travelling and moving around you undoubtedly developed into a professional in your job. You had to, otherwise the organisation or company would not have allowed you to continue. New assignments are waiting for you—maybe not as a managing director but perhaps as a specialist, a project manager, or a professional in a specialist area.

It is possible that retirement is waiting for you or offered to you by the organisation or company you work for. That can provide you with even more freedom and independence to plan, together with your partner, your next new assignment. You may accept an assignment to assist another company in a new project, or you may choose to realise ideas or dreams that you have had together with your partner for a long time. Now is the time to execute these plans. Your new activities may range from running a camping to writing a book to babysitting your grandchildren to rebuilding your house or apartment. There are many activities from which to choose. As an entrepreneur living abroad, you have to take the initiative yourself. Do not sit and wait; create together with your partner your own future. You can influence that more than you think. Finally, you are your own boss, and you should decide yourself.

It should be a nice experience to finally be able to think about what you are going to do when your last assignment as an expatriate comes to an end. Do you have the choice between taking an active retirement or accepting another job offer? What will your next steps be? Where do you want to settle down? Do you want to go back to your (maybe forgotten) roots? Have you made up your mind or do you just want to look for a new place to live? You could maybe rent a summerhouse or buy a holiday home and take the time to decide later. Put your furniture in storage and be free to decide later? Or for instance rebuild or restore a house or an apartment that you bought a long time ago as an investment and make it your new, permanent home.

Having travelled for twenty-four years, we realised that we had become used to moving and having sometimes two houses or apartments to live in. Retiring meant for us that we became restless, as the hectic period of moving around was over. We could not stay in one place—however nice and beautiful it is—and we decided to rent a second apartment, so that we could move between the two places whenever we wanted. Some people who are not used to living a hectic life, like we lived before, may not understand this, but this is our method for keeping fit and staying alert. We may change later on and get really settled, but the restlessness is a consequence of the life we lived.

Spending quality time with grandchildren is a new direction that many people in our situation take and that they enjoy very much. We now see the results of our five children having been brought up to travel around with the outcome that some of them also have started to move around and take up international positions and have international marriages. We created a very diverse and intercultural family. So just to visit one of your grandchildren, to drink a cup of coffee or have tea with them, is not possible, as all of them are living in other countries. It makes no sense to us to settle down close to them, as most of them will continue to move around. They must live their lives and we must, too. Luckily, it is possible to maintain good contacts thanks to the Internet, Skype, and other communication systems. We find it especially enjoyable on the one or two times a year that we visit in person and see them in real life.

Whatever you choose to do, it should be a new and fascinating period in your life.

# CHAPTER 6

## Let Our Children Speak

### 6.1   Suzanne

Looking back now I can only say that I've had a very privileged life as an "expat kid", with lots of experiences and opportunities that most children do not get. When it all started, however, I had quite a different opinion.

I was thirteen years old when my parents decided to move to Spain, and I had just started high school. All was going well; my grades were good, and I had a secret crush on a neighbourhood boy. I did not need a change in my life. Besides, we had already moved about quite a bit in Holland, and it felt good where we were at that time. So, I was not very happy when the announcement came, which I think was at the end of 1987. Why would they want to mess up my life?

If I remember correctly, I did let my parents know my dissatisfaction, and I do not think I was a very easy kid to handle at that time.

But, when I got to tell the news to my friends and in school, some excitement developed. It was, after all, not something that happened very often in the village. I had to take private English lessons with my brother, as we would be going to an English school, another source of excitement.

When the pictures of our new home, with a swimming pool, were shown, I was "sold". Yes, there was still the issue of saying goodbye to friends, but the excitement prevailed.

Then, the moving company came, and everything had to go in boxes. Like I said, we had already moved a few times in Holland, so this process was not new. Still, it was different this time, and it gave me a thrill.

The moving truck was going to take some time to get to our new home, so as a family we drove to Spain by car, with a few stops on the way so that we would not get there ahead of our stuff.

It was the summer of 1988, and it was the start of our new life.

There are so many good things to remember about the different places that we've lived in and visited. The five years in Spain, Switzerland, and Denmark had a lasting impression on my life. And perhaps the most striking change was that while in the beginning the trips back to Holland were something to look forward to—to eat French fries, *frikandel* (snack), *drop* (liquorice), and *hagelslag* (chocolate sprinkles) and to meet up with family and acquaintances—after a few years, those trips became a drag, an obligation.

I could write about all of the adventures that we've experienced as a family and the adventures that we are still experiencing when we all meet up somewhere in the world, but I would like to tell you three stories that have stayed in my memory about our time in Spain and Switzerland:

Just arrived in Spain. Mom and Dad thought it a good idea to spend a day at the beach like we used to do in Holland. So we decided to drive to Valencia, the coastal city. Leaving Madrid sometime in the morning, by car, we started the trip. On the way it became clear that distances in Spain were a little different . . .

We arrived in Valencia somewhere around dinnertime. No day at the beach. Just a quick look and a long drive back home . . .

Think of Spain as a very hot, desert-like country, around Madrid.

That is what I thought in the beginning. It came as a surprise when, not more than an hour away by car, there were mountains and snow, with a local market. And they had *churros*, a Spanish snack that at that time was not widely known outside of Spain. Every country had things to discover.

After two years in Spain we were going to move to Switzerland for the next three years. We found a home big enough for our family. The only issue was the location. Maarten and I had to go to school by train and bus, leaving our home in our nice little Swiss village at 7 in the morning to get to school by 8:30 a.m. It just goes to show that sometimes the international school is not close by. However, fortunately, the three-year stay got cut short. In the summer after the first year in Switzerland Dad got a new job in Denmark. We had to move and start a new school within two months. That was a bit of a rush. There were no goodbyes to schoolmates, and it was a quick move.

To describe the effect that my overall experience had on my character and personality it is better to skip straight to the day that I returned to live in Holland and started studying at university.

In the summer of 1993, I was back in Holland to start studying in Rotterdam. It was a city that I did not know, but that was not the difficult part, as I was by now used to exploring a new city. The difficult part was—besides the language—being on my own and not knowing anybody.

The experiences abroad had taught me that the best way to move ahead was to just go ahead: go to the university introduction programme; go to the student associations; go to meet new people. I knew that I needed to adjust to my new situation. I knew that I needed to look for all of the good things in the new environment and to not dwell on the negative aspects. Of course there were moments when I would have liked it if I had had my parents living closer by, just like there were moments when I did not enjoy the country we were in, but those moments passed, and new exciting developments took up my attention, back when I was in a foreign country and now that I was on my own in Holland.

The foreign experience has changed me. Adapting to new circumstances and making the best of it have been valuable lessons. But there have also been challenges. At first, entering

*What Changed Our Lives*

into a long-lasting relationship was not easy, because in the past we had always moved away after a few years, and it was easier to keep a relationship somewhat superficial. I also sometimes get restless, because I long for new excitement. But, in the end, all those experiences have given me what I have now, which is a wonderful husband and two loving daughters—my own family with whom to experience new adventures.

Lastly, I wish to share with you a few words from my husband, particularly about his experiences with his family-in-law in different countries.

## Arjan

When I first met my parents-in-law it was for a very brief moment. They came over to visit their daughter who was my girlfriend at that time. I don't think we spoke much; they left again the next day. Apparently, it was quite normal to travel all that distance for just a single afternoon. Later, they invited us to come over to Switzerland to join a party for their other daughter; I must have done something right.

At the party I met the entire family, and they were all talking a different language. Some were even mixing all sorts of languages, but nobody seemed to notice. I found it very hard to follow any of the conversations, but I had a great time and certainly enjoyed all the food and wine. Later, I realised that everybody was telling what he or she had experienced in the last six months or so, and that this was probably the first opportunity to share it through conversation.

At first I thought it was a bit strange, but later I realised that it was just different to what I was used to.

Since I met my wife, I've seen so many different places, because her entire family just can't stay put for a while. Nevertheless, I enjoy every moment I spend with my wife's family. There's always a good story to tell and many things to see.

## 6.2 Maarten

I remember very well our first steps into the expat life; one night my father came home from work and gathered us around the table to discuss moving to Madrid, Spain. At the time it seemed like a really cool thing—moving to another country. I was twelve years old . . .

Then started the preparations; there were additional English classes, as I would be attending an international school where the English language was the norm. There was the realisation that the moment of final goodbyes was closing in, followed by the finality of the move itself.

It is not easy to start again, to start afresh without anything familiar, compounded by the isolation of not being able to speak the local language.

So what do you do?

Initially, you turn to that which is familiar, which is your direct family—those who made the move with you. They will form the base from which you will start re-building your life.

Step by step, you start adjusting to your new surroundings and to the local culture and start picking up on the local language. By the time that you start school, the feeling of isolation should be beginning to slowly disappear.

A new school and new surroundings—both filled with new people who you do not know and who are speaking in a language that is not your own. These are daunting odds to overcome. However, soon you will realise that most people in the international schools come from similar backgrounds and have similar experiences to your own. This bridges the gap very quickly, and you are absorbed into the normal school life.

So what happens?

Within your direct family, you will forge different kinds of bonds. Your family members are the constant in an ever-changing world, as you move from country to country and from school to school. It is not a bond of sharing your innermost thoughts or feelings; it is the knowledge that no matter what, they will be there for you (as they have always been), and that gives a certain added dimension—a comfort.

Moving around, with the continuous change that that brings, forms families of individuals. We are not close, in the literal sense of the word. We do not see one another very often, and we do not communicate with one another regularly. However, when we do see one another, there are no uncomfortable silences; we pick up where we left off without stepping out of sync . . . .

In terms of other relatives, such as aunts and uncles, and with regard to friends, you will most likely experience a loss of contact, despite best intentions. Your life experiences and interests are completely different, and it will be difficult to find common ground. It will result in short, generic conversations, filled with the usual clichés and followed by silences, in which neither party really knows what to say.

In school, you will adapt and fit in quickly; you are surrounded by people with similar backgrounds and experiences. You learn to adjust quickly to new situations and the ability to form new bonds quickly and say goodbye to the old ones.

The friendships that are formed are relatively platonic and almost never reach a deep level, however, as you will both know that the time for him or her or you to move on is around the corner.

We learn to adjust, adapt, and overcome. Consequent of always changing situations and the multi-cultural environments of the international schools, you develop a form of flexibility and openness to other cultures and experiences. You will lose your prejudices and preconceptions of different countries, cultures, and people. You will develop that ability to always find a common ground from which to move forward and to face challenges; you will gain self-reliance and a willingness to plunge into the deep end.

There are those who say that it is not good for a young person to be taken from his or her roots. Or that you can only move around until your children reach a certain age. Those children should have a base.

Ultimately, it is different from person to person and from family to family. In my personal opinion, I am a better person for it. Moving around has given me the opportunity and privilege to experience other cultures and to develop in different directions. It has taught me self-reliance as well as the flexibility to adjust and adapt, the ability to blend in. It is different for each person or family. Each individual needs to assess whether they are willing

*What Changed Our Lives*

to exchange the known for the unknown to jump into the deep end. I, for one, am grateful for the opportunity that I had, and if I had the opportunity to go back in time then I would do it all over again; I would not change a thing.

## 6.3　Frank

"Hi, kids, do you have the time for a family meeting?" Once those words were spoken by our father we knew what time it was. It meant that change was going to happen. The big surprise was always, where to next?

How do you describe the experience of growing up in five different countries all around Europe? It is a life that some dream of, but it is also a life that some have hated. It is a life of mixed emotions, of many hellos and just as many goodbyes. It is seeing new places and learning new languages; it is about expanding your mind and opening your thoughts as well as your heart. When our father said that he wanted to write a book about it, it made us all (I believe) realise a lot of things, as we had probably never put on paper before. Hope you enjoy the reading as you go through the minds of five different children all experiencing this road at different ages.

### The Beginning . . .

The expat life for me started at the age of nine. We were at that time living in Klundert, the Netherlands, and life seemed pretty normal and routine—going to school, playing with the neighbours in the playground around the corner, being up to acts of mischief (if you would like to know more details, please do not hesitate to contact the local fire brigade), and growing up in a small town, where everyone knew everyone else. It all started with the move to La Moraleja, Spain. There were mixed emotions and lots of excitement.

We moved during the summer holidays and into a house with a swimming pool. I guess this was all so new, and home was soon forgotten. This was our home now . . . We had all said goodbye to our friends in the Netherlands, and we were curious about our new school. This would be the first time going to class in English. It was a challenge at first, extra classes just to learn how to pronounce "th"—as in "think", "three", and "there".

The great thing was that we were not alone. The international school catered to hundreds of children who were experiencing the exact same thing. This made making friends easy, and it allowed for quick integration into the school system. As I am also one of five children, I was never alone. We all pulled closer together, as we were in this together; we became friends before anything else. Of course, we had our fights and arguments, but at the end of the day we were coping together.

Madrid was an amazing experience, and, strangely enough, while it is the longest ago, some of the memories are the most vivid. Retiro Park, Prado, Plaza Mayor, and the international school with its huge grounds, separate buildings for the junior school and the high school; all things that will never be forgotten.

At this time, we were learning English and Spanish simultaneously. This seemed impossible at the time, but, years later, I realise that a lot of it stuck. During the moves after this, learning the local language became a sport, enjoying it very much.

After Spain, we moved to Switzerland and then to Denmark, and after this to Sweden. That is where the journeys as a family stopped, at the age of eighteen.

It is like a bug, like a virus infecting your mind, the curiosity of where we were going next was huge. The excitement of packing all your things and unpacking them in a new room, new house, and new neighbourhood. For me this feeling never stopped, it was a new adventure each time. It just left a lot of questions: What would the new school be like? Any kids to play with in the area? What would the new house be like? Will I be learning another language? How long will we be staying this time?

Thousands of questions for a kid at any age; all would be answered in time.

The life was never boring. It never got dull, it was amazing! Here are some of the pros and cons of the expat life in the way that I experienced it.

## Brothers and Sisters

You hear many stories of brothers and sisters not getting along; however, when leading the type of life that we did, they are all you have. They are the ones who are in the same boat as you, going through the exact same things. An advantage being that we were five, this meant there was always someone to play with, to fight with, or to talk to. Of course, we did not always all get along, kids are not supposed to. But the bond was strong, and as we all got older these bonds grew stronger. Nowadays when we meet one another, it is like we have never been apart. This is an amazing feeling. We have experienced so much together, and we have so many memories together that there is always something to laugh about. Thanks to my brothers and sisters, there are still many stories to talk about over a good glass of wine.

## Schools

What seemed to be difficult in the beginning became easier as time passed. The realisation that there were thousands of children doing the exact same thing made it somewhat easier. The goodbyes were not easy, but it became something that was part of your life. You were, however, more and more careful about making new friends, not sharing your feelings with just anyone, and often not letting your guard down in order to protect yourself. I would not say that I built a wall around myself, but relationships with the vast majority were on the surface, and the number of real friends I had was minimal as you hoped to keep in touch when the time came. That the time was going to come to say goodbye was inevitable, so no time was spent talking about it. Then, when it came, addresses were exchanged, and that was that. Unfortunately, many friends were lost, especially the ones from an early age. Due to the Internet these days some can be found again.

## Languages

As I grew up, my interest in learning the local language grew, and the challenge to learn as soon as possible was happily accepted. Among us siblings, English became the mother tongue, and it even became the language spoken around the house. The attempt by our parents to keep our mother tongue intact was soon given up. The fun began when we, the kids, tried to explain to our parents that an "f-word" does not really mean anything . . . Not an easy argument for a bunch of kids, some of whom were going through puberty.

## Mom and Dad

The stronghold of the family! As the moves became more frequent, communication in the family became more important. A family meeting took place before each move, asking all if they were in favour of the next move. This was essential to being able to live this kind of life. These moves also resulted in a different type of relationship between my parents and me. Thank you for being there! Here is a little poem that depicts the relationship with my mom and dad. (I'm not sure if it is still hanging in the toilet.)

5 years old—My parents can do everything! They are the best!

10 years old—Mom and Dad don't really know everything!

15 years old—Mom and Dad don't have a clue!

18 years old—My God, they are old fashioned

25 years old—Let me ask my parents.

35 years old—How would my parents have done this? They always had some good advice!

50 years old— . . .

Thank God that I can still ask them, and they are still willing to give advice.

## Looking Back

What sort of better life could you have wished for? How do you describe this to other people? How do you tell your story without sounding stuck up and arrogant? Who understands what you have gone through? What you have seen?

I guess nobody does understand the life that you have lived unless they have done the same thing. When I talk about my past to my current friends, some understand, and some look confused and ask why?

I could not imagine my life any other way. What I have learned during these years has shaped me forever. It has opened my mind, it has allowed me to experience different cultures and see different countries. It has made me independent and has given me the ability to quickly adapt to new surroundings—a great advantage in today's fast-moving, global economy.

## Leaving the Nest

At the age of eighteen I left the comfort of the family nest, starting my own adventure. Where did it take me? It took me to the hotel school in Switzerland, where I remember being dropped off at my dorm room with nothing more than a suitcase. The hotel school was like all of the other schools that I had attended since it was small, one big international community. This made integration easy and quick; all that I had experienced just seemed to fit in, it was all familiar. At eighteen, I was a young adult, and the life that I had led had made me independent. I knew how to do my own laundry, tie my own ties, even how to iron my own shirts. This could not be said by many of my classmates.

During my studies, the urge to see the world never got any less. The bug that we had been infected with as kids was deeply rooted in my own personal plans for the future. I wanted to see the world, working my way through the ranks of the hotel industry.

My last internship led me to Orlando, Florida; this year was to change my life forever. It is there that I met my wife. After a somewhat tricky start, we embarked on our own adventure around Europe, moving from the Netherlands to Belgium; we are currently living in Berlin.

## Present

Now, at the age of thirty-five, married and with two sons of my own, it is impossible to imagine the task that my parents took upon them. Keeping us all together and going through the motions with us. It was just as new for them as it was for us, but they needed to keep their cool and control. They never appeared stressed or nervous facing the next step in our lives together. It has shaped them as much as it has us.

The years of moving have allowed me to see many things, but it is the continuous support of our parents that has made me the man that I am today. It is them that have taught me to be flexible, independent, and ready for change. It is their guidance throughout these years that has allowed me to continue on my own journey.

## Conclusion

After these many years of moving to many different countries only one thing remains to be said: If you can, do it! It has been an amazing experience, and it has made me a global citizen, ready for any challenge that is thrown my way. It has made me restless and curious as to what else is out there, wanting to discover the world. Going on vacation is one thing, but living there, working there is an entirely different story. It teaches you that you can live without *hagelslag*.

Mom and Dad, Suzanne, Maarten, Irene, and Paul, I thank you for sharing these amazing times with me. Although nowadays we are dotted all around the world, the bonds are still strong. I miss you all and look forward to the next time that we can all share a glass of wine together. Cheers!

## 6.4 Irene

*Introduction*

Life as an expat, with a large family, has been the most nourishing experience of my life until today. I started this journey when I was six years old by moving to Spain. I don't remember much from this move, just the beautiful home that we had in Spain and my first move into an international school. Unfortunately, we didn't stay there long, and after two years, we moved to Switzerland. But, wait, it continued from there—onto Denmark, Sweden, the Netherlands, Russia, and then Switzerland for my college years.

We weren't just an expat family; we were a family with five children, all at different stages of our lives. My first move didn't mark me that much, since I was still young. However, let's say that from our move from Denmark onwards, when I was going through puberty, the expat life started to have its effects.

Moving from country to country meant of course the changing of houses. Finding a suitable home for a family with five children was not always an easy one. I remember visiting these beautiful (and also some not-so-beautiful) houses; it was always a time of excitement. Since our parents always wanted to give us a fair chance of picking the best bedroom of the house, we always got to take turns (with the master bedroom being of course off limits). The eldest sibling got to choose first, with our first move away from Holland. My turn came up when we moved to Denmark. I remember coming into this huge, high-ceilinged hallway, with a nice staircase up. At the top of the staircase was *my* room. It was huge, with a large window that overlooked the garden—it was great. When I chose this room, it was made up just to my liking—all "girly", we could say.

I was about twelve years old when we left Denmark and moved to Sweden. The most important thing in every move was always finding a school for each child. However, our parents always found the best international school we could go to.

I will try to explain below, to the best of my knowledge, my feelings, views, and experiences, both negative and positive, of my expat life.

## Positive Aspects

Being an expat, to me, means a constant exposure to new and different cultures. It is the most nourishing and the best learning environment for a child to grow up in. You are continually challenged and are continually introduced to people who come from the other side of the world but who at the end have the same views as you. They teach you about their experiences of growing up, their family traditions, their religious views, and their family heritage, which you then automatically compare to your own. You become a sponge, just taking in all this new—knowledge that, at a later stage in life, will help you tremendously.

Since most of us were all going through the same things, we became very close. I would always depend on my siblings and parents first, rather than a friend I knew from school. I have the closest bond with my youngest brother, since we moved the most and stayed the longest together. Even now, if I have an issue or a secret to share, I would share it first with my family rather than my best friend.

In my opinion, it's not just us, the children, who have changed; my parents have also evolved. I could say that I am very close to both my mom and dad. I am comfortable in speaking with them openly, no matter what the issue. In my experience, I have come to realise that I tell my mom things that my friends would never dare share with their parents. I have always felt so open in speaking with my parents, especially my mom, since no matter what I say, they have always supported me and have never judged me.

The constant moving around and the changing of homes and schools makes the family relationship a unique one. It bonds people in a way that is hard to put in words.

At this moment, in 2013, we are all spread around the globe; however, we are still as close to one another as always. The communication between us may be lacking now and then, but

*What Changed Our Lives*

I know that if I have a problem then I can speak to my family, and they will be there for me. We have made a small tradition where we all try to meet up every five years in celebration of my parents' wedding anniversary, and, so far, we've been doing quite well at keeping that tradition alive. I, personally, need to see my family as often as I can.

When we do meet up—all seven of us, plus wives, husbands, nieces, and nephews—it seems like our relationships with one another have never changed and that we aren't living as far apart as we are. The conversations and discussions between us just continue where they left off. For me, it is the most enjoyable and amusing of times that we share, especially since we have grown into different people though still have that continuous bond of accepting and supporting one another.

## Negative Aspects

For me, the hardest aspect of an expat life would be not having a home, no roots that you are bound to. Since you are constantly moving and are making new friends every couple of years, you have no place to go or call home. For me, personally, this was a difficult one. Though I must say that my parents did everything in their power to make sure that we felt at home and comfortable in our environment.

Sometimes, you become jealous of the people you meet who have known their friends since birth, whereas I never had this chance; I was making new friends every two or three years. Even when you move, you promise to keep in touch; however, this is not often the case. The funny thing is that the people I have met were usually jealous of me, because of my constant travelling around Europe and seeing new things. This could cause some negative reactions, in regards to the fact that I may have been considered snobby, just trying to explain where I was from. In that case you learn very fast to whom you tell your adventurous story, and to whom you don't.

The idea of having a Dutch passport loses its value in my opinion, since I do not feel Dutch at all. Since I have lived in so many countries, I have lost feelings with regards to my actual nationality; I have adapted to each culture that I have lived in. This makes explaining where I am from very difficult. Also, when I do visit the Netherlands, I feel like a tourist and do not even speak the language fluently. I would say that I feel more at home in Switzerland, since I have lived there the longest.

Another point would be that you do become very independent at an early stage of your life, meaning that you can usually manage by yourself, and you do not need people to help you. This can cause you to be an outcast of certain "groups" in the schools that you go to. All the international schools that I went to, I found it hard to place myself within a certain group. You become somewhat a loner, where you do not really need many friends; one or two close friends usually suffice. Until this day, this is still the case, where I stick more to myself instead of having a huge social network.

## My Journey

After my last destination with my parents, which was Moscow, Russia, I decided to move to Switzerland to start my studies in hotel management. During my college years I met many people and made many friends who had a similar background to me, which made me feel less of an outcast.

I settled down in Switzerland for about nine years until I decided to bounce around again, first to Indonesia and then to the Maldives.

My final destination, for now, is Dubai, UAE, where I met my husband (who also has an international background). I am currently expecting a baby.

I must say that now that I am going to become a mother, I have decided that I wouldn't mind exposing our future son to the same experiences that I had. It matures you in a way that you would not expect. In addition, I sincerely hope that I will have the same relationship with my child as my parents have with me.

## 6.5   Paul

Being the youngest in our family, I had the privilege of being able to stay abroad the longest. I was two years old when we first moved, which means I had a slightly different experience than my older siblings. Currently, I do not have many memories of my early years of travelling; however, this does not mean that it has not affected me in some way. There are many different arguments that can be made about the benefits and hindrances about leading an expatriate life. I will be highlighting personal points, both positive and negative, which will hopefully show a different perspective to that of my brothers and sisters. They will show that the age at which I started the expat life had some effect on my personal development.

## History

First, I would like to give a brief history of the moving sequence, showing the ages at which I moved. I was born in Roosendaal, the Netherlands, with both parents being Dutch. This means that I am a Dutch national through and through. When I was two years old we moved to Madrid, Spain. We stayed there for two years and then moved on to Penthalaz, Switzerland, where I attended a kindergarten. After one year we moved on to Copenhagen, Denmark. This was the first time that I went to an international school. After three years, we continued our Scandinavian tour and moved to Stockholm, Sweden. Here I once again attended an international school, which soon became the norm. Three years later we moved back to the Netherlands, but this time to the northern part, to a place called Haren. Even though I am Dutch, by this point in time my language had suffered, and I attended an international school once again. After another three years we moved to Moscow, Russia. This is where I attended high school, also in an international school, and it also proved to be the time when I left my parents' side. After four years, at the age of eighteen, I moved to Sheffield, England, to study. I spent five years there and then moved on to Bluche, Switzerland, also for studying purposes. Even though I spent three years on studies there, six months of that I spent in Manchester, England, for an internship. After my graduation, I moved to Amsterdam, the Netherlands, where I now reside.

## The Benefits of Living an Expat Life

The first response most people give when I mention my history is, "*Wow*, you are so lucky to have seen all of that!" And I would have to agree with them. Having been able to see so much at an early age

*What Changed Our Lives*

gave me many positive attributes. I have selected a few of them and elaborated on how they have affected me.

## The Cultural Influences

The great thing about Europe is that you do not have to go far to experience different cultures, and so although we always stayed in Europe, I still got the opportunity to see and learn different cultures: the Mediterranean styles of Spain to the Nordic countries of Denmark and Sweden to the neutral Switzerland to the liberal Netherlands to the island culture of Britain and to the former Soviet Union, Russia. On top of having actually lived in these countries, I also went to international schools in most of them, which means that I was subject to even more cultures in these schools. This has allowed me to see how different people from all around the world interact and behave and in the end all get along together under one roof in school.

Today, I can honestly say that because of my interaction with all of these cultures, whenever I meet someone, I respect them for who they are without having any prejudice. It has also taught me to be open to everyone no matter their history. It has affected my communication skills as well, such as in how I approach people from different cultures and what is acceptable and not. This has grown into something of a fascination of different cultures, and when I meet people from places that I have not visited or have not met any people from before, I am always curious about their natural habitat and cultural practices. Currently working in the hospitality industry, this gives me a huge benefit since the hospitality community is always diverse, and I have seen that I am able to gain the respect and trust of all those around me no matter where they are from.

## The Effects on Personality

### Adaptability

Having resided in so many countries, I have grown proud of the fact that I am able to adjust my attitude and behaviour to my surroundings and blend in with the local community. This came from going out and actually meeting people from the community and not remaining isolated in the expatriate community to which I also belonged. Even though I may not have been able to speak the language, in every country that I lived I had local people come up to me in public areas to ask for help in terms of directions and such, even though generally one would not approach a tourist to ask for directions. This approach has led me to learn quickly about my surroundings and adapt myself to the norms of the surroundings. I have been able to use this skill to my benefit in my professional life as well, as I learn quickly and am able to adapt my norms to the different departments in the hospitality industry.

### Independence

Having left my parents' side at the age of eighteen and moving to Britain alone, and after that to Switzerland and the Netherlands again, shows that one can grow to be independent with a diverse history. What I mean by alone is actually the physical fact of moving alone. I did have the support from my family, but this will be discussed in the following section. From what I have encountered, a lot of people fear moving, which is understandable because they leave their comfort zone. Having never really developed a comfort zone, I am comfortable going wherever I want without hesitation. Another factor that has an effect on one's independence would be that moving around a lot means that when you get to a new country, you do not immediately have friends, so you become comfortable doing things on your own and do not rely on others to do things you want to do, and this has an added bonus that you will meet people in doing so.

The Family Bond

Like I mentioned above, when moving around with your family you become very supportive of one another. This grows, because having an international background means that you experience the same things as other members of your family. So when moving to different countries and maybe not having so many friends in the beginning means that you can always rely on your family, who will always be there. Since in most cases you will attend the same school with at least one of your brothers or sisters, you will always find at least one recognisable face in the crowd. In the present day, my family is spread around the world, and we do not see one another very often, and the communication between us is not always the best. However, I do know if that I ever have an issue and need advice I can always call any one of my siblings or my parents and the ensuing conversation would not be an uncomfortable one; in fact, it would be a conversation as if we had had one the previous day. This arises because we all know we would be there for each other because we always gave that support to each other when we were in foreign countries together.

## The Negative Aspects of Living an Expat Life

The expat life is not all positive; there are always negative points that can be made, and it is not an easy life to get into. The following are some personal experiences that I feel are linked to the lifestyle we had. These negative aspects are all linked to life after the expat stage since I can only think of positive things during the movement, and I am only able to see the effects of the moving in the latter stages in life since I was too young before that.

## The Emotions

Moving around means that there are a lot of goodbyes involved. Since I started at a young age, I am getting used to this, but it does bother me in an emotional manner, and it may affect others. What I feel happens is that since we all know that we are going to be moving on once again, we close ourselves off to certain things. This is because there is no need to get too close to anyone since in the end it just makes the goodbye harder. This makes it sometimes difficult to open up to people. This can be a problem at times. However, there are ways around it. During my schooling years I had only a handful of friends in each school. This let me open up to them. In my current state I still struggle to open up to people, but I feel that I am learning and improving.

## Isolation

As I mentioned above, the feeling of isolation is also caused because it is increasingly difficult to keep in touch with the friends that I have made throughout my life. This meant that when I arrived in a new country I would have no friends at that point in time. This varies from people who do not move because they have friends and acquaintances that they have had their whole life.

Which means that the first couple of months after a move are the most difficult due to this feeling of isolation. Having such a rich history makes it difficult to connect to other people since you are able to speak of a multitude of experiences compared to others. And if one does start talking about it to others it can be conceived as bragging, even though this was not the intention (this is perhaps why expatriates tend to group together).

In my personal experience, I have lost touch with my roots, and even though I am 100 per cent Dutch, I no longer feel like one. So with my move back to the Netherlands I treated it like any other move to another country since I do not know much about the history or the current culture. This has affected me in some rather unexpected ways since people see me as Dutch, and they do not understand why I do not know about certain things, such as the geography of the country or the history of the royal family. This has led to people saying that I am not Dutch and has actually made me once again feel more like an expat.

## Conclusion

There are always pros and cons to every action in life. Personally, I would not change a single thing in my life. I have thoroughly enjoyed my time so far, and I do plan to keep on moving around the world and seeing more. Since I was only two when I first moved this has become the norm for me, and I would not know how it would feel to settle down in one country. Even during the five years that I spent in England I started to feel uncomfortable and had a feeling that it was time to move on again. For me, the positive effects far outweigh the negative aspects, as they all have become part of my life. The advice I can give all of those people who are considering starting an expat life is to consider the solitude of their family and that if they do try then they need to understand that the first few months will be difficult and that full disclosure with the whole family is key. One has to understand that they all become one another's anchors.

I want to close my story with a positive experience.

Having moved around so much, I have met a lot of people, and you never know where you may meet them again. In high school in Russia, I met a guy who had gone to school with me in Stockholm five years before. In Geneva, I encountered an old teacher of mine, a coincidental meeting that almost caused me to miss my flight. And, most recently, in Amsterdam, going to a cinema with my sister, I met a guy I used to be in class with in Russia, along with his sister, who used to be in my sister's class; we now regularly meet up for a drink. All I can say is that it's a small world.

# CHAPTER 7

## Citizens of the World

At the end of a working life, the circle is complete. The children are married or are living with partners, and they have jobs in different parts of the world. They have grown up into citizens of the world. The world has become their place, and if they want, they can settle anywhere to live and work.

When speaking to others, we found that not everybody understands this way of life. Some people seem to think that it is strange that we managed to live our lives in this way. We can understand that, but as you have read in Chapter 6 ("Let Our Children Speak"), this is the way that our children experienced it. We were lucky that we could do it and that we could offer it to them. We took the chance to do so when the opportunity was given. Others would not have done it the way we did or simply could not do it. Some people take only one or two assignments and then go back after that to their home country, maybe for the studies of their children. That is everybody's choice.

Let us be fair, sometimes it is not a choice as the circumstances did not allow moving around; or other elements played a role in making the decision not to go for an expatriate position logical in a particular situation.

For me, as an expat, having such a position for a long period of time, you keep on moving around, because you have lost your roots. But what is against that? If you see that as a threat, then move back. If not, continue. You have it all in your own hands! My wife and I are still restless; we are flexible, and we feel that we could live everywhere. But we have had to find the right balance ourselves. We have fewer friends left, that is true, but on the other hand, the Internet nowadays helps a lot to get to know the whereabouts of lost friends, so contacts are renewed. It is a fact that we have fewer real friends, but we can live with that aspect also. We have accepted it.

I would like to conclude that this small book—*What Changed Our Lives: An Expat Adventure*—is written about our family. We together decided to take the challenge to move and to work and live as an expatriate family, never realising that the journey would be one of twenty-four years' duration. We realised that it would not be easy, and it would not always be as sunny as it may seem from the outside. We had our problems of course. The children had issues at school, doing homework, and in the normal growing-up stages. We, as parents, were often busy with our demanding jobs, and we did not always give enough time and attention to our children. We were a normal family like everybody else in the country. The moving around, the cultural differences, the languages, and the international schools made the difference.

To summarise the ideas that are written about in this book:

Good preparation is needed before you decide to take a position abroad.

Decisions have to be made with regard to taking one or more assignments, the choice of international or local schools, and the role of the partner.

With a move abroad you have to understand, accept, prepare for, and adapt to cultural differences.

I hope that potential, new, and established expatriate families can make use of some of our experiences. Have a good and safe journey.

We enjoyed it, and we are grateful to the company who gave us these opportunities.

Rudolf Hartong

*What Changed Our Lives*

# "CITIZEN OF THE WORLD":
## A SONG BY ELLIS PAUL

Reproduced below are the lyrics of a song that was sung by one of our children in an international school.

# ELLIS PAUL

## Citizen of the World

I'm an American

Was born of Scottish blood

I got a Frenchmen's eyes and ears

I got the walk of a British thug


There's an African in my skin

Seminole are my kin

I'm a man of a thousand faces

Many nations, creeds and races


I am

I am

I am

I am

I am

a citizen

I am

I am

I am

I am

a citizen

of the world

of the world

of the world

of the world

of the world


Blue September day

Sky came tumbling down

Living in a world of hate

Crying at heaven's gate


Our nation's a tougher one

Muslims, Jews and Christians

Father Michael says a prayer

Whispered up into thin air

I am

I am

I am

I am

a citizen

I am

I am

I am

I am

a citizen

of the world

of the world

of the world

of the world



Scarecrow in an oil field

Soldier in the sand

Seeds of violence

Seeds of peace

What will grow in the holy land

If I could talk to Ghandi, talk to Christ

Talk to Mohammed, ask advice

Oh Saint Theresa, MLK

We need your advice

Cause it`s judgement day


I am

I am

I am

I am

a citizen

I am

I am

I am

I am

a citizen

of the world

of the world

of the world

of the world

Copyright Ellis Paul-VanceGilbert-Sharon Teeler

Ellis Paul Publishing, SESAC

Disismye Music, ASCAP

Note: I obtained the copyright permission to publish this song on July 1, 2013.

# ABOUT THE AUTHOR

Rudolf Hartong was born in 1947. His education is in human resources, and he worked for forty years in human resources and general management positions—twenty-two in the former and eighteen in the latter. He worked in the Netherlands as a human resources professional until 1988. After that, for the following twenty-four years, he and his wife and their five children lived in seven different countries, where they encountered and experienced various cultures, religions, and situations that changed their lives.

Having retired in 2012, he has written this book based on his and his family's own experiences in the hope that it can help new expatriate families in their decisions and preparations for working abroad. Existing expatriate families will probably recognise the situations that he describes and realise that they are not alone.

Rudolf and his wife currently reside in Switzerland.

For comments and remarks, you may contact Rudolf via email: rudolfhartong@yahoo.com

You can follow Rudolf on his blog: www.rudolfhartong.com

www.ingramcontent.com/pod-product-compliance
Lightning Source LLC
Chambersburg PA
CBHW030912180526
45163CB00004B/1799